let

the

rain

fall

let
the
rain
fall

lauren cohen

gatekeeper press
columbus, ohio

let the rain fall

published by gatekeeper press
2167 stringtown rd, suite 109
columbus, oh 43123-2989
www.gatekeeperpress.com

library of congress control number: 2020940221

isbn (paperback): 9781662901928
eisbn: 9781662901935

this book is dedicated to everyone
who helped me find my voice.
now i want to help others find theirs.

to find your voice, i encourage you to write in
the margins, underline passages that speak to you,
and take any notes you'd like.

this book is for you.

tell your story.
shout it. write it.
whisper it if you have to.
but tell it.
some won't understand it.
some will outright reject it.
but many will thank
you for it.
and then the most
magical thing will happen.
one by one, voices will start
whispering, "me, too."
and your tribe will gather.
and you will never
feel alone again.

—l.r. knost

to my future self,

i hope by now you have learned more about yourself. i
hope you have begun to gather the pieces to fit your life's
complex, yet beautiful puzzle. at this point, there is still
so much missing, and yet, there is so much you already
understand. you developed a passion for writing and i hope
you have continued. i beg that you publish your work in
the near future if you haven't already. i hope that as you
read this, you realize how many accomplishments you have
made in oh, so many different ways. you are an activist, an
advocate, a writer, and a leader—not just today, but every
day. you always will be. this is your power.

—lauren, age 14

each and every word, meaningless
until you choose to give it meaning

let this be our story
our collectivity as one
authenticity, so deeply raw

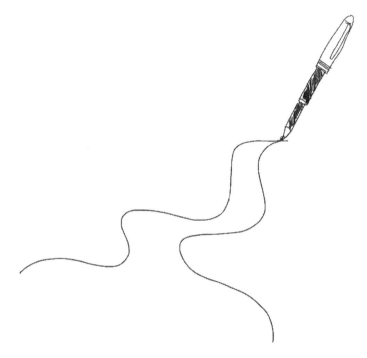

i struggle to know what i should write
all i know is that my chest feels tight

these are the moments where i feel my breath being stolen
my lungs close
and all i can hear
is the sound of my own silence

i light your candle every day because your fire is everburning
a light in a world that often feels so dark
a light to the heaviness that shapes this world's arc
a light that so profoundly fills my heart
you are the light
from which i'll never be apart

the pain of longing grows deeper as my heart gets weaker

my love for music transcends the boundaries
by which sound can be identified
when sounds are combined and intertwined
to produce rhythmic harmony
this expression of emotion is art in every form
music takes me to a world where sound is reborn

you may be a phone call away
but the telephone lines are pulling us
farther and farther apart
all i ever wanted was simply your heart

we fall in love with fantasies
because they are easier to conceptualize
for we fear what reality brings in disguise

i fell into love with you as quickly as you fell out of it
why do we allow ourselves to fall short for love?
we accept less
we deserve so much more

we never seem to fear the flu
because we always know what to do
using bandaids to cover the real wounds of society
is what i struggle to conceptualize
those very bandaids won't heal
the way self-remedy does
no aid can fix our broken bones
only our shattered pieces can come together
to find peace

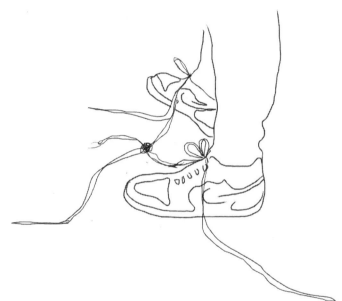

don't play my feelings like they're hopscotch
i won't ever let you step over me

you say you love me with every fiber of your being
but what i feel for you is submolecular
if only you understood the depths of what i feel for you
no microscope can capture the beauty of your intricacies
you are beyond the boundaries of science

your absence haunts me
like thoughts
that enter my mind at midnight

the rain from the sky
the tears from my eyes
pouring down like waterfalls
yet that's nothing to despise
for it is society that normalizes one's understanding of pain
and this flawed perception brings down the rain
we must understand that in order to grow
life's painful seeds we must sow

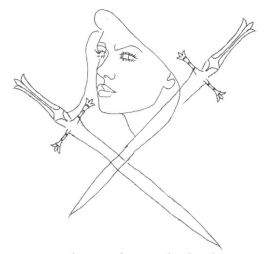

why is it that our bodies become so immune to violence?
don't expect me to be your soldier
i must first be my own warrior

.

we say rest in peace
despite humanity seldom achieving it
it's a paradox of sorts, huh?

my soul wants to hold yours as if time was not a construct
and instead

limitless

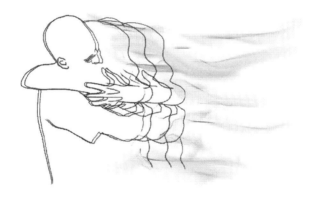

broken heart, not a broken soul
this pain is not linear
allow yourself to
feel the depths
just to find its height the next day
soon enough, peace will come
it is on its way

they call us cowards for not knowing our own power
            never fear your own strength
                    because
            we are all simply flowers
            in a world full of weeds
        aching to find our own peace

        our power is within ourselves
            waiting to grow and heal
        our perceptions may be different,
                radically, at times,
        but knowing power in collectivity
    is a sign of strength in a world full of weeds

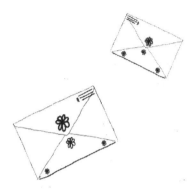

a letter of love to
the marginalized, the ostracized
those so often criminalized,
the eyes in which we set aside
for the real love we feel inside

the unknown used to scare me
but i found peace in not knowing
uncertainty can lead us to our greatest clarity

the world may feel unsettled, yes
but isn't that inherent to our existence?
our humanity lies within not knowing
and from that, i find ease

are devils real?
she's an angel in disguise
masked with a lightness so foreign
to this world's heavy weight

you claim that i fulfill you
that i am your other half
but love, you cannot be whole
with dependence on two
for your wholeness comes
from you and only you

my mind is a symphony
so complex in every way
that no one *dares* to bring me out of sync

we sit together in the moonlight
hoping that the music
will stop the world's fight
against us

what if i'm subconsciously conscious?
cognizant of my own cognizance

our society continues to shame
and blame
those who never asked
for this pain

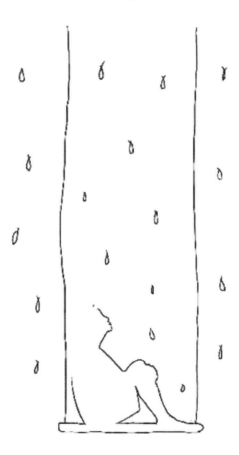

does my expletive tone help you understand that
i am not okay?

i am not okay

and that in itself is okay

we have no sense of direction
so we let the waves shove us
back and forth
against the shore
until we can feel no more

she locked you in a dungeon
and threw away the key
don't think she's coming back for you,
the decision was left to me

she slipped a note behind the bars
read it when you can
once you take the time to look
you'll know your relationship is banned

i believed you.
i trusted you.
i loved you.

it was all too familiar
i had heard this before
i gave you my life in exchange for more
but there is nothing left for me to give
i put all of my energy into you

now it is time for myself
i need to love me
the way i loved you
before

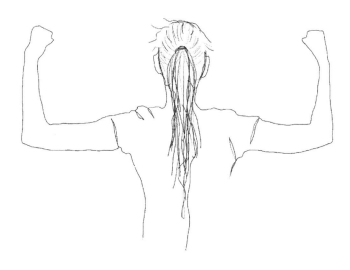

the future looked familiar
she had seen it once before

the words left me broken
i was close to tears
i am trying to be open
i can feel the spears

the metallic taste in my mouth
left me feeling empowered
maybe it was fate
i was used as bait
and to indoctrinate

it was too late.

let's
       fight
           for
              our
                   rights

          in the middle of the night
             with no lights
           or feelings of spite

life is one large mountain
together we will climb
using words to flatter
as we ascend through time
together, every step we take
leads us down a different path
just one mistake we make
brings us a terrible wrath

if we work hand in hand
to reach the peak of the mountain,
then we won't be stuck in the sand
all that will be left is a fountain
full of tears of joy and misery

oh, what a life we are living

words like raindrops falling from my mouth
my heart aches but my soul roars

dreaming in a field of bitter herbs
aching for some sweetness

i know i'll find peace with
you and only you
your rawness like no other

the spark in her eye
set a fire in the sky

touch me
hold me
play me like the strings of your guitar
play each cord delicately but passionately
let me be more than just your summer song

i am your muse
i am here through it all
just please,
please don't fall

i thought i saw you standing at my door,
but i mistook you for the shadow of your ghost
you are no longer my dream
but my nightmare
one that finds a way to stick with me
permanently
within my soul
you are the nightmare tattooed on my heart
i can't erase you
you are imprinted
this is my permanence

they say wisdom comes with age, but really
it's the experience, the loss, the bruises, the pain
that make you rich with knowledge
no number, no age will make me strong
i've climbed mountains, fought wars
and saved myself enough to know
that strength is ageless

why is it
that we pride ourselves on honesty
but refuse to truly be authentic?
we must tell the whole truth
and nothing but the truth
yet we lie to ourselves
we say everything will be alright,
that the pain will heal
when we know it won't,
not completely
an honest person builds an honest society
authenticity is what we need

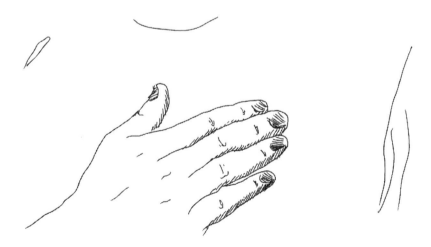

i'm your shadow
the one that follows you
but i must be my own silhouette

when i'm with you
it's like i'm learning the alphabet for the first time
each l e t t e r
and each word
requires attention to create a sentence.
i will learn the alphabet 100 times just to say
i
love
you

you say you want simplicity
i'm antithetical to what you want
i am complex, i am nuanced
my depth causes confusion
so don't go around asking for simplicity
when i fall in love with you for your complexity

the first step to fighting apathy is passion
she wanted to feel nothing
and instead, she felt everything
every touch, every bruise
all she wanted was to find a fuse
to burn away the pain she felt
each and every day

she hated the objectification
and the hypersexualization
i am not an object, she said
to be pulled by the strings like it's your puppet show
no more gratification

democratize the systems of enterprise

the origin of nothingness is simply being.

being whole in a world trying to pull me apart
into pieces, bits and pieces
not realizing its internal meaning

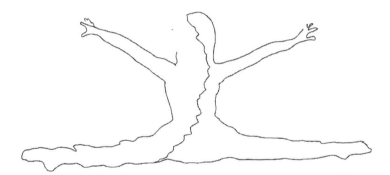

... george floyd.
ahmaud arbery.
breonna taylor.
michael brown.
tamir rice.
trayvon martin.
sandra bland.
danye jones.
emmett till.
stephon clark.
philando castile.
christopher deandre mitchell...

and every black community whose heart was stolen
by systems of oppression
and by the very people who claim to protect
the most marginalized

we, the people
of the united states of america,
divided by hate and bigotry,
claim to be the land of the free
when oppressive is all we'll ever be
unless we reform and restructure the systems,
by which we'll see
a need for justice and racial equity

uncertainty:
it's okay to not be certain
it's okay to lack clarity
it's okay to just be

—making sense of the nonsensical

everyday injustice does not call for everyday silence
we are looking for simple answers to complex problems
when we must uplift and amplify
grow, not simplify
the systems that must be redesigned

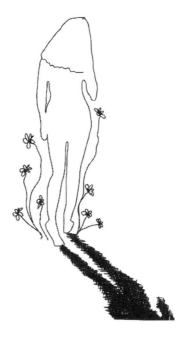

the length of her skirt was not consent
why is it that *you* thought yes instead?
no indication of acquiescence, and yet you *violated*
the very place she called her sanctuary
her body is a temple, so treat it as so

it's no longer a difference in political opinion, but rather morality
one's right to exist is not partisan
not left
not right
simply humanity's fight

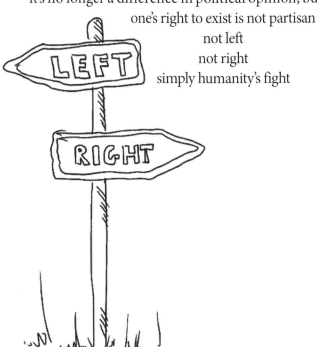

still waiting for the day when being black
no longer means a death sentence in this country
systemic racism is real and present, institutionalized
not simply a foundation of the american settler state
but has manifested itself in far too many brutal ways
you go to houses of worship to pray
but do you pray for the black lives being taken
each and every day?

the notion of civilization stems from the question of civility,
or lack thereof
it is one's own task to decide civilization's civility,
so which is it?
tell me

raindrops pour from my eyes
the colors are all divine
rivers and streams galore
oh i miss who i was before
take me back to the days
when the pain didn't stay
and the rivers and streams
were only dreams and dreams
let me see the world with lenses
then i'll observe with my senses

the sight
the touch
the sound
the taste
the smell

the raindrops have dried up
all that is left is a large cup
filled with rivers and streams
that will forever stay with me

i am not a dove
i cannot speak
i'm not one to love
i am quite weak

i don't try to hate
i sing my mind
i'm not your fate
i am one of a kind

i live to dance
i don't like to stand
i'm not one for romance
i am trying to understand

i don't play games
i wait for no one
i set the world in flames
i play in the sun

you taught me something
you allow me to see
i am no longer bound up
i am finally free

123

the impact of human connection is far too powerful
often, we become so isolated in our own worlds that we forget
what it means to touch and to love

there is profound power in being able to appreciate
the human mind and soul
love one another
spread radical empathy because all we've got is each other

at the very moment that you are reading this,
children are laying on concrete ground
in internment camps, trying to sleep
with the fear that they will never see their parents again

may we recognize what's happening at the border objectively

it is our responsibility as americans to condemn
the human rights violations taking place,
if we have to wait for migrants to die
due to our flawed immigration process
for there to be an outcry,
then we are completely lost as a nation

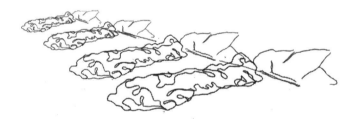

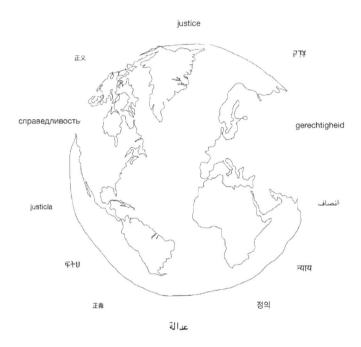

our fight is the same in every language

we strive for equality
we rise for opportunity
we lie in the arms of ability
these are the words that fall out of my mouth
like a broken piece of pottery
i am shattered and cannot be put back together

my childhood friend was groped at the age of six.
she was then raped at the age of ten, and again, and again.

this was the day my life changed forever.
the day i realized i could make a difference.
this was the day i fought for her justice.

this is the story of a twelve-year-old girl
learning that her childhood friend was raped.
this is not the story of a twelve-year-old girl
staying quiet and sitting down.
i rose up and i fought, i'm still fighting.
i am fighting for all that have ever been abused.
i am fighting for minorities and priorities.
i am fighting for the people of this earth
who have yet to receive their justice.
change is coming and i am part of it.
—lauren, age 17

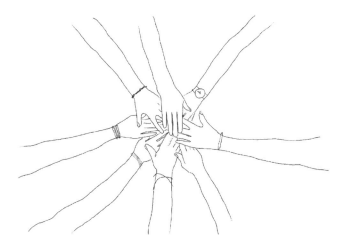

tzedek, tzedek, tirdof
justice, justice you shall pursue
—the torah

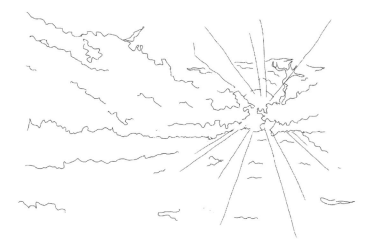

the sun always shines after the rain

acknowledgments

i am eternally grateful to everyone who helped me put
this book together. to rob price and the team at gatekeeper
press, thank you for helping me turn my dreams into a
reality. to peta mckenna, thank you for taking my poetry
and making it sing with your beautiful illustrations.

to my parents, thank you for believing in me and
my work. to my mother, kim, and to my father, ron,
thank you for your endless love and support, and
for always encouraging me to express myself.

to my friends, thank you for sharing your stories with
me and trusting me throughout the years. thank you for
standing up with me, and working towards a better future.

to my teachers, thank you for giving me a platform
to find my voice. to oak hall for supporting my
education, my endeavors, and my creativity.

to everyone who has a voice that has been oppressed
or underrepresented in society, this book is for you.

lauren cohen is a social justice activist and advocate
who uses social media and other forms of expression
to mobilize action and establish a dialogue on the
issues affecting society. poetry provides a vehicle
by which lauren navigates through the complexities
of the issues plaguing her generation.

through her poetry, lauren reaches out not only to her
peers but to society as a whole. her poems seek to uplift
the voices of those marginalized and left behind. lauren's
poetry reflects her own efforts to confront human struggle
and the intensity of emotions associated with this struggle.

peta mckenna is an artist and designer from perth,
australia. having recently completed her masters
degree in fine arts from the university of florida, she
plans to pursue a career in set design, film and television.
peta has an extensive range of artistic and creative
abilities which she utilizes across several disciplines
including woodworking, drafting, painting,
and illustration. www.petamckenna.com.

Manufactured by Amazon.ca
Bolton, ON